What's Under Your Rug?

What's Under Your Rug?

Esther Renee' Daniels

Titus Works Publishers
www.titus2empower.com

For ordering information please contact:
Titus Works Ministries
www.titus2empower.com

Book Coaching by Dawniel Winningham
Edited and Formatting by: Allyson M. Deese
Layout: Marvin D. Cloud

Michelle R. Harden, Branding and Marketing
Coach www.whateveryoudobrandyou.com

Earl Duncan, Cover design by:
Regal Standard Web & Graphic Designs,

Rekeda Rianna, Photography
http://papillonperspectives.showitsite.com/

Author fashioned by Sofistafunk Skirt Co.,
Arlinda MacIntosh,
www.sofistafunk.com

Printed in the United States

I dedicate this book in loving memory
of my dear cousin:

Lori Theresa Woodson

09-11-1966 ~ 06-06-2005

Enjoy your peace!!!

CONTENTS

CONTENTS

ACKNOWLEDGMENTS

First and foremost, I thank God for using me as a vessel to manifest this book.

Secondly, I want to thank my husband Andre' Daniels for his love and support as I journeyed through this experience. Then there are some really special people who shared their knowledge, time and resources. I will be forever grateful to you for your love and support.

I also give thanks to the following individuals, who without their contributions and support, this book would not have been written:

Carla Cuney

Daniel V. Woodson

Jeri Gardner

Johnnie Breakfield

Pastor Natalie Francisco

Aqua Copeland

Blewett A. Wright

FOREWORD

In reflective contemplation, King David considered his life and declared, "Behold, You desire truth in the inward parts, And in the hidden part, You will make me to know wisdom" (Psalm 51:6 NKJV). In each of our lives, there is the need to look inward and assess our past to recognize how it affects our present and future. Esther Renee Daniels provokes us to look under the rug of our emotions and not only uncover hidden issues, but resolve them by removing the power they have over us. Her life is a testimony to what God can do in your life when you seek truth in the inward parts.

Facing her own personal battles in the past, Esther is a living example of an overcomer. We can individually relate to her life's story and recognize our own self-limitations. We are inspired to succeed in life and to continually live in true victory.

—Mia K. Wright,
Co-Pastor,
The Fountain of Praise

PREFACE

Esther Renee' Daniels takes on the importance of doing our work to heal old wounds and trauma in *What's Under Your Rug*, her debut book. Renee's work in the field of spiritual empowerment and her work as a theologian have garnered the attention of hundreds across the country. From her work with *Titus Works* on-line ministry and monthly conference calls to her local work with a Texas-based ministry, she is an important voice in the spirituality movement.

What's Under Your Rug offers valuable insight on maintaining our emotional and mental health amidst the stress of everyday living. It explores America's obsession with "looking well" while going through life as a wounded soul. Renee's new book also addresses how things that are under our metaphorical rug often interfere with our personal and professional growth and evolution. As someone who had the honor of witnessing Renee's journey of transformation and healing, I know that *What's Under Your Rug* is not just a book. *What's Under Your Rug* is a personal testimony to the power of doing one's own healing work and how this work can literally align us with God's purpose for our lives.

Readers of *What's Under Your Rug* will experience a down-home, real-life story of one woman's healing experience, as well as straight-forward guidance on how anyone, man or woman, can uncover, discover and discard the things keeping us locked in spaces that block our progress. In my humble opinion, this book should be required reading for anyone embarking on a career of spiritual teaching, social work, human services and emotional recovery.

I'm excited and elated to write the preface for the first literary child of Esther Renee Daniels—minister, teacher, healer and friend. I am sure God will bless every word and every page of this spiritual guide to personal healing and empowerment!

—Ifalade Ta'Shia Asanti

Award-winning journalist and author-
*The Sacred Door: A Spiritual Guide to
Power Living*
www.tashiaasanti.com

Prologue

I grew up hearing many different sayings. Possibly, you have as well. But there is one saying I don't think I really understood until I became much older. That saying went like this, "You shouldn't just sweep things under the rug." I must be somewhat of a literal person, because when I think about the saying, I literally see someone with a broom sweeping dust or dirt under a rug. But as I experienced life more, I realized this saying is not what I envisioned it to be.

One thing about what I initially envisioned is part of what the saying implies. That is the things of life we attempt to avoid or act as if they do not or never existed, becomes the dust or dirt of our past. We often sweep this dust or dirt under our own personal rugs of the mind. With the hopes of never having to acknowledge it again, we believe if we don't look, it doesn't exist.

So, my question for you dear reader is, "What's under your rug?" What have you attempted to sweep away in the hole of forgetfulness? What have you refused to admit to yourself or anyone else, took place in your life? This sweeping thing we do can be devastating and harmful concerning how we live our lives, in the decisions we make and the people and things we allow in our lives. That is exactly what I did in my life. I pretended certain things did not happen or they did not matter.

I found later that they did matter. Sweeping those events of my past did not make me better; they actually made me sadder. I became really sad about being me, and because I was ignoring what I swept away, I could not understand why I felt the way I felt. Nor did I realize that day by day my self-esteem was being swept with it.

INTRODUCTION

I was given an assignment to write a book and I thought to myself, *this must be me saying this, surely God would not be telling me to write a book*. I thought this because I had just attended a women's Bible study and we had an author as a guest speaker. Since I had just listened to her speak, there was a good chance that this idea to write a book was coming from hearing her story.

Plus, what would I have to write about anyway? I am not an expert on anything; what could I possibly write that would inspire or help another human being? So, I did what most people would probably do—I disregarded the thought of the potential of a book. But like any assignment that God gives me, it would not leave my spirit, therefore, I began to pray about it. Seeking God's opinion on this book, I remember praying, *"Okay God, if this is truly what You want me to do, then would You at least give me the subject matter?"*

Shortly afterwards, it was revealed to me what God wanted to say to you through this book. He wants you to be healed in every area of your life. He wants you to know that what He said through David in Psalm 147 is real,

"He heals the brokenhearted and binds up their wounds."

He wants to bless us with the freedom to experience the joy, peace and happiness we so desperately desire to experience. In order to write this book, it meant I had to write about some things in my life that, of course, I didn't want to. However, not only does He want to free you, but He wanted to free me as well.

ONE

Uncover What's Under the Rug?

In June, 2005, my cousin committed suicide as a result of not being healed from the things she suffered. For years, she was obsessed with this love/hate relationship she had with two significant people in her life. She loved them both but hated them for the type of relationship she perceived them to have apart from her. She was unable to come to terms with not being able to obtain what she craved from these two people and it tormented her. The sad thing is, she already had what she longed for—she was just unable to see it or feel it. Mainly, because she could not give to herself, she could not receive from anyone else.

There's an old saying, "You must first learn how to love yourself before anyone else can."

3

What a true statement. Yet, it's hard for those of us who suffer in this area to understand that it is impossible to feel love, or recognize love from others, if you don't love ... first.

As the years went by, my cousin became emotionally and mentally ill. It came to the point where demonic forces physically took over her. One night I called her to check on her and I became convinced that demons are real. Through our conversation I experienced something I will never forget, and through that experience, the desire to not see anyone else suffer from emotional and mental sickness began to weigh on my heart.

Today, so many people suffer from all kinds of different issues that they are trying to sweep under the rug and act as if they do not exist. The more dust that is swept over that rug, the worst the inside becomes. So much dust has been accumulated that the issues begin to ooze out in our behaviors, in how we respond to people, in the decisions we make, in the people we allow in our lives, and more importantly, in how we treat ourselves. God is saying it is time to stop hurting hurting yourself and others. He wants to show you how to live beyond the hurts of your life, but He needs you to do some things for deliverance to become a reality!

The first step in being healed is to find out what is making you sick, and look at it square in the face. The reason issues are swept under the rug is because in our subconscious mind, we believe if we don't mention them, if we don't think about them (which is impossible), they will go away.

Wrong! They never go away. As a matter of fact, they grow bigger and bigger, as if they take on a life of their own. What does that mean if you are dealing with several things under your rug? You have all of these different issues fighting to see which one is going to have control.

Here is the hard part. The only way I can give you an example is out of my own experience. As a child, I was molested continously by a girl. I was so afraid to tell anyone what she did to me, because I did not know what happened to me was not my fault. So for years, I wrestled with this violation, and no matter how hard I tried to sweep it under the rug—not mention it, or not think about it—it would not go away. Well, guess what? The voice in my head became louder and louder until one day it was so loud, it screamed, "Don't you just want to die?" Up until that point that particular issue effected just about every decision I made, because it told me, "I was ugly, I was a bad person, I did not deserve anything good." I felt so unloved.

I didn't suffer from low self-esteem, I didn't have self-esteem or self-worth. I had nothing with substance to hold on to ... my life felt so empty and worthless.

Years later, I thank God for allowing me to know what I know now. Otherwise a recent event could have affected me in an unhealthy way. I am a Facebook junkie, and while reading some of the posts on my wall, I kept seeing the name of someone who was celebrating their birthday. I kept saying to myself, *that name sounds familiar, I know this name.* So, after trying to figure out where I knew the name from, I finally clicked on the link and when it opened, it blew my mind. It was the person who molested me as a child. *Wow,* I must admit it rocked me for a minute. I thought about that for a few days. But I came to the conclusion I was truly grateful for the work that had been accomplished to help me find a way to live with this unresolved issue.

When I was little girl, around elementary age, I would spend most weekends with my grandmother who I am named after, Esther Mae Guillory. She has gone home to heaven and I miss her very much. I *never* doubted her love; I knew without question, that she loved me. Every weekend I would go to her house and play with the children in her neighborhood.

The person who found it necessary to violate me lived two houses down from my granny.

I trusted this person. I believed what she said. I never would have imagined she would hurt me in any way. That is why I walked around for years feeling guilty about an act that was *never my fault*. However, I did not know that and for years I wanted to die as a result. This is where and when, how I felt about myself began to develop.

I thought I looked like a dirty, bad, ugly, fat, broken, liar, nasty, black gal (which is what my grandfather, who meant the world to me, called me) and that had to mean I was ugly, right? To top all of that off, somewhere in my being I just knew God was not pleased with me. Everything I thought about myself after that violation was negative, all because I believed I allowed this event to happen in my life.

Had it been the only life event under my rug without resolution, that Facebook encounter could have been a horrible experience for me. This proved even more to me how important it is for me to handle those events that take place in my life. Even if taking care of them is only how I handle them emotionally and physically, that's enough to live and let live.

If you are trying to live life with the mentality of the "don't mention it, don't think about it, it will go away" belief, let's take the power away by uncovering what's under the rug.

The first step in doing that is based upon what has become one of my favorite quotes from Socrates: "An unexamined life is a life not worth living." You must examine your life—look at those things you have tried to hide from yourself and the world.

I hear you. "Why is it so important to drag up stuff from the past that don't have relevance to what I am doing today?" That's a sweep under the rug statement! The things we have ignored from our past affect what we are attempting to do today. Those things have partially or completely blocked us from performing to our highest potential.

Melody Beattie, the author of *Journey to the Heart*, says, "Some of the pains and illnesses we suffer from are indications of acute physical problems. They're signs that our body has broken down and we need medical attention. But many of the aches and pains we experience are symptoms of a deeper process—a process of healing and cleansing our heart and soul." Therefore, these very things keep us from moving forward when God speaks.

Because of old messages, old beliefs and old habits, we stall when we hear or think we hear a message from God to move in a certain way. Stalling is about a few things; one is fear, and another is insecurity. Some of it is about reverting back to a negative message from the past. Is it not relevant? I say it is very relevant and I can prove it through my own life. It took me 20 years, (don't tell nobody) to get my bachelors degree. Twenty years! Why? I am glad you asked.

It took me that long because of fear, insecurities and reverting back to negative messages. These were not just negative messages I heard from others, but messages I gave to myself. Oh, you thought this book was only going to be about pointing fingers at someone else, in order to explain why you are the way you are? Nope that's not where we are going! I told myself on many occasions that I was not good enough or smart enough to finish this awesome task of receiving my degree. All as a result of one subject, Algebra! I took my first algebra class and failed it, so I had this bright idea that maybe I needed to go back to remedial math and refresh some things. Guess what? I failed remedial math! I was convinced that I was stupid. Who fails remedial math? And truth be told, I failed it twice. I was so convinced that I would not be able to complete this class, I began to take a class here and there, with the hopes that one day my curriculum would change and I would not have to take a math class. That never happened.

I thought I would try again. I signed up for my second algebra class, but had to drop it in the middle of the semester because I informed my professor I did not have a clue what he was talking about. He suggested that I take intermediate algebra, and I did. There isn't a grade for that class. I finished it and enrolled in my third algebra class. I am embarrassed to say, I still could not grasp the concept. However, it was the only class that was stopping me from graduating. I would like to say I was sticking to it because I refused to quit, but the truth is, I was hoping God would give me what I needed to make it through that class. On the day of my final I went to class and took the test.

After I finished, I walked those wrong answers up to my professor and looked her straight in the eyes and said, "I have done the very best I can do." She said, "I know you have and I know you are tired of us torturing you." I obtained a "C." God gave me what I needed. That was the happiest "C" of my life! That episode happened over a period of years, due to my fears, insecurities and old messages I gave myself.

We must address the fact that we sweep issues of life under the rug. I have learned from this whole experience, just because I may not think of what has wounded me every day, does not mean I am not affected. This ability to not think of something allows us to feel like we have gotten over that thing while it is silently attacking us from the inside out. We must attack it from the outside in. Through prayer, guidance, and courage, we must fight back and not buy into the lie that there is nothing there.

Here are some steps and thoughts you need to consider to get started in this fight:

1. When you look back over your life, what would be the first thing you would write down that resembles your rug? Remember it does not necessarily mean there is just one, ask God to reveal to you everything you need to see right now.

2. Remember it could be a person, an event, an entity, or even you.

3. Sometimes there is a mental block, but here's a way to jog your memory that is really easy. Pull out your year book(s) and the stuff you are trying to forget will most likely reappear.

NOTES

NOTES

TWO

Name the Dirt and Dust That has Been Swept— Uncover, Discover and Discard

You are probably wondering, *how do you name the dirt and dust that has been swept,* and *what does it mean to uncover, discover and discard?*

To uncover is simply a matter of raising up the rug. It means picking up the mats to those places in our hearts where we have swept the hurts and the pains of our lives. Why would anyone want to do that? Good question... FREEDOM!

Freedom from being haunted and controlled by unfinished business. As I was writing this, a Scripture came to me, "And they overcame him by the blood of the Lamb and by the word of their testimony..." (Revelation 12:11).

This verse says a lot to me, but most importantly, it speaks to an important aspect of our lives that is paramount to the kingdom of God, our testimonies. If we do not uncover that which satan has been using to keep us bound, then how, or better yet, what do we testify about that we have overcome? The blood of Lamb was for everything we experienced, not just those things that scream so loudly we can't ignore.

The fight today is much greater than us overcoming gossip, lying, cheating, stealing and cussing. This fight is about those things that have been swept under your rug that makes you gossip, lie, cheat, steal and cuss. Those things don't just happen in your lives because the words exist, they happen because something inside of us is saying something that makes you feel uncomfortable about YOU!

The question is; do you want surface freedom or deep-cleaning freedom? Deep-cleaning is the kind of freedom you have that when you walk in the room, you can hold your head up, not because you want people to *think* you got it going on, but because from the inside out, you do have it going on! That cannot happen without uncovering what is keeping you from living a life of freedom from inside of yourself. Maybe we need to look at the true meaning of the word freedom. Webster defines its meaning as, "the state of being free; exemption from the power and control of another; liberty; independence. *Made captive, yet deserving freedom more."*

This definition is power-packed. Look at the first part of the definition, the state of being free. We have all desired to have this in many areas. Yet, when there is an opportunity to achieve this kind of freedom, why do we turn and run the other way? I believe part of the reason is due to not wanting to take on the responsibility of doing what's needed—naming those things that have you bound.

The second part of the definition says, "exemption from the power and control of another." This part gives me a little problem in that it appears the door has been opened to blame others for not having freedom. This could be an aspect in some cases. On the other hand, could it be that we have used that as an excuse? In fact, it is often due to being in denial, being unwilling to even acknowledge that which haunts us, and knowing what is wrong but looking in the wrong direction for relief.

Finally, look at the last part of the definition, "liberty; independence." Each time I read the word liberty I automatically reflect on what the Bible says in 2 Corinthians 3:17 in the King James Version, "Now the Lord is that Spirit: and where the Spirit of the Lord is, there is liberty." Don Egan states in an internet article, "So freedom from all pain disease and sickness is within our grasp. Let us then, like the woman who came through the crowd, touch the hem of his garment and believe we receive our healing." The way to this freedom is to name those things that are causing us the most pain. If you really want to be free you must stop sweeping and hoping it will all go away, because it won't.

I know what it feels like to walk into a room but must first prepare myself to do it. I would be afraid of what someone thinks of my appearance. *Can they see the weight I have gained? Is my hair right? Do I belong here?* I would have a conversation with myself and would examine every negative thing I felt about myself from childhood to adulthood. Those very things have kept me home on many occasions, missing out on life because of old messages I have lived by. Don't get me wrong, there is nothing wrong with wanting to look your best. It becomes a problem when that consumes your decision to step into the room or not. I heard a statement at one point in my life that makes a whole lot of sense. The person said to me, "You need to stop judging your insides by someone else's outsides."

In the Bible there is a story that most people have heard about the Samaritan woman, (John 4:7-30). As I was reading it, two things stood out to me. First, Jesus informs her, "If you only knew the gift God has for you and who you are speaking to, you would ask me, and I would give you living water." What Jesus says to her excites me because it tells me that God has planned way in advance to give me gifts. If I could hold on to that thought, sweeping under the rug would not be my option.

Someone said to me recently a profound statement: "God's first gift to us, His VERY FIRST GIFT was when He made us in His image!" WOW think about that. His very first gift was making us in His image. Will someone please tell me why we feel so inadequate, useless, not enough, unrememberable, unworthy, shameful, guilty, and resentful, just to name a few? If we are made in God's image, we need to realize He doesn't feel any of those things. Often, we lack a very important aspect of our lives—confidence. We don't have the confidence to realize that no matter what is under that rug, God's got us, and He is going to walk EVERY step with us to work through it. Jesus said, "If only you knew the gift God has for you." How many gifts have we missed because our eyesight has been clouded by depression, sadness, detachment, isolation, fear and ultimately, lack of faith? It is time to pull that rug up and let whatever comes out ... out!

The second thing that leaped out at me was this unnamed woman's response when she leaves Jesus. "Come; see a man, who told me all things that ever I did: can this be the Christ?" WOW! Do you see where I am going with this? She had an encounter with the Lord and *what*? She walked away asking, "can this be the Christ?" Are you kidding me? Really? Seriously? Can this be the CHRIST? After reading this in one version, I thought *maybe this version stated it this way, let me look at another version* and guess what? In every version it does not show her running away with surety that it was the Messiah—she was still questioning if it was Him or not.

Isn't that much like us? Because we don't feel whole and complete we are always asking a question to determine what gives us the sense that something is missing. If we could just remember the *very first gift* that God has given us, there would be no need for questions. In most sermons preached about this woman, we are lead to believe that she ran away from Jesus proclaiming the good news, and in some aspects she did, but I still have to ask, did she? After all she did run away asking a question not stating a fact, and the Bible does not talk about this woman again for us to know what change, if any took place in her life. I don't bring this up to dispel the way this passage of Scripture has been taught for years, I bring this up because that is what I did over and over in my life. I would attend something many times, join things many times, hoping that something would fill the hole I had in my gut. The one where the wind would blow right through me and chill me to the bone. The one that constantly reminded me I did not measure up. Even today I sometimes find that hole questioning whether someone remembers me or not.

I remember the exact day I met my First Lady and mentor, Mia Wright. I remember where we were and the conversation we had. Every time I saw her after that day the first thing I would say to her is, "I don't know if you remember me or not, but my name is Renee Daniels, we met at Walgreens." The first few times she would lovingly say, "Yes, I remember you."

Then finally one day I saw her, and greeted her as always and her response was a question, that blessed me way beyond what I knew. She said, "Renee', what is it about yourself that makes you feel that I would not remember you?" I wondered, *WOW how often do I do that?* I

NAME THE DIRT AND DUST THAT HAS BEEN SWEPT

am worth remembering, but why did I not think so? I realized I didn't have any confidence, or self worth; as a matter of fact I walked around most of the time with my head down, looking at the ground. A friend of mine noticed that about me and gave me specific instructions. I was told, "When you get out of your car, hold your head up and look people you pass straight in the eye and say, 'Good morning,' 'Good afternoon, how are you?'" That was one of the hardest things I had to do.

I thank God for friends who love me enough to help me see the beauty God has placed in me. We all have struggles in life that could make us feel incomplete, but the Apostle Paul says we can be filled up to all the fullness of God. In Ephesians 3:14-21, the Apostle Paul made an awesome statement or prayer for spiritual growth. This prayer if embraced can make the task of discovering those things that have convinced us that we need to hide them away, can now have the rug pulled off of them. The verses read as follows:

> **14** When I think of all this, I fall to my knees and pray to the Father, **15** the Creator of everything in heaven and on earth. **16** I pray that from his glorious, unlimited resources he will empower you with inner strength through

---
22   *WHAT'S UNDER YOUR RUG?*

his Spirit. **17** Then Christ will make his home in your hearts as you trust in him. Your roots will grow down into God's love and keep you strong. **18** And may you have the power to understand, as all God's people should, how wide, how long, how high, and how deep his love is. **19** May you experience the love of Christ, though it is too great to understand fully. Then you will be made complete with all the fullness of life and power that comes from God. **20** Now all glory to God, who is able, through his mighty power at work within us, to accomplish infinitely more than we might ask or think. **21** Glory to him in the church and in Christ Jesus through all generations forever and ever! Amen.

What blesses me in this prayer is when it tells me, "Then you will be made complete with all the fullness of life and power that comes from God." Is that a blessing or what? It tells us that we can become full and whole. So what does a whole person look like? Pastor Charles Stanley of InTouch Ministries stated it as follows: "They are generally satisfied with life. They feel loved and are able to love others in return. Difficulties and hardships don't devastate them, because they are able to go through them with the confidence in God. They are not complainers or someone who is quick to blame others. A positive attitude guards their mind since they know that the Lord will work everything out for the good. Listen, many times being a Christian doesn't automatically make us feel complete. Fullness comes only when we experience God's love for us."

Now I know you are probably wondering *why is she talking about all of this?* Because this non-confidence kept me from allowing God to fulfill the blessing He had ordained for my life. Who could I possibly minister to with my head looking at the ground? Since I did not trust anything or like anything about me, how could I believe what God may have been saying to me? Like the Samaritan woman, I was walking around questioning, could it be God, really? I made no decisions without the approval of others. I can remember sermons I wrote that I would not preach until someone read them and confirmed that they were good enough to preach or teach. Everything I did was based on someone saying it was okay to do it. Who was I going to minister to like that?

One thing that made me feel not worthy to be in your presence, not worthy to believe that God was actually talking to me and giving me instructions, was living my life based on past experiences. Those experiences proved in my mind that God didn't want to really talk to someone like me. Someone who had been where I had been. Come on, why would God give instructions to a recovering drug addict and alcoholic? I knew he wanted me to help others find out that they did not have to live like I once lived. The only thing that had really changed was that I was not doing drugs anymore nor was I drinking alcohol. Although my behavior was not like the ones that went along with drinking and using any more, it was still weighing me down with tremendous guilt. It's like this: The pounds you gain while eating chocolate don't go away just because you stopped eating chocolate. I was still left to deal with the damage I had created during my disease of addiction. I still have nightmares and memories I wish God would wash from my brain.

I became sober on March 3, 1988 and at the time of this writing, I'm celebrating 24 years of sobriety. The reason I believe God wanted me to talk about confidence is because had I not started the process of removing one onion layer at a time, I would not be in a position to be used in the manner God planned to use me. I am no longer asking, "Is this God speaking to me?" I know it's God!

So if you are trying to look the part or act the part it will be so much better and rewarding when we allow God to search your heart. . .because then He will reveal to you what's holding you back from accepting His love and His blessings for real. Then your mentors won't have to work so hard. You will trust God's voice when you hear it rather than seeking someone to confirm what you believe God is speaking to you!

The things that I did not give much attention to are the very things that made me feel like there was something wrong with whom God was trying to create me to be. Therefore, to uncover is much more important than what most people think. I know, why dig all that up? Because if you don't, you will be buried alive with it. Set yourself free. Yank the rug up and expose everything under it to the *Son*, oh that just came out, I meant the sun. First let's look at what freedom means for you, give that some thought, then write what that looks like.

1. First let's look at what freedom means for you, give that some thought, then write what it looks like.

2. Now that you know what your desire is for freedom, this next task might give you a little more willingness to do it. Write a list of anything that comes to

your mind from your past, that when you think of it you feel discomfort.

Now what happened in these discomforts? What do you remember about each one of them.

NOTES

NOTES

THREE

How has the Sweeping Affected Your Life?

I guess you are now wondering, *how does she expect me to figure out what affect has the sweeping done that has taken placed in my life?* You are right if you are thinking this is not going to be an easy task. If you are thinking this might hurt, again you are right! If you are thinking this might change some people in my life and more importantly change you. Getting an understanding of the damage created by what you have experienced through sweeping certain events under your rug is something that can change everything about you. Your values may change your perception of what you habelieved most of your life. How you make decisions will change and your motives for the decisions you make will be different. This understanding will do for you what you have not been able to do with all the other things you have tried. You may be the person who has found yourself using outside things to sooth those ill internal feelings in your life. What are outside things? Things like drugs, alcohol, food, sex, shopping, hording, isolation, sleeping, and depression, just to name a few.

We don't really see the manifestation of how these outside things affect our lives until it is either brought to our attention or they bring too much pain to continue using them Listen, it is not normal to do drugs, it is not an extra curriculum activity. Using drugs of any kind is a tool people use to avoid the real them. If you think prescribed pills are not a part of that, please know prescription drug use has risen all over the country. Pain clinics are popping up all over the city, and trust me people are not attempting to manage pain from injuries, but more so to manage inner pain. This inner pain is a product of not facing life as it comes, the issues we have decided we did not need to look at, and just swept under the rug. The reason we continue to use these tools, because they are mechanisms that work to keep us from feeling. One day the tools stop working!

I know this because it happened to me. There was a time in my life that everything

I thought was "no big deal," became more than a big deal. It became a HUGE DEAL! It became so huge that the day came I wanted to die. But prior to that, I was one who used many things to soothe what I did not understand. When I was in high school, I started using speed and my excuse was to manage my weight. Mind you, I was not fat, but that is what I saw in the mirror. I desperately wanted to change who and what I saw of me. I wanted so badly to be someone else, and look like someone else. I could not see what everyone else could see, and therefore the experiences I had endured to that point were slowly eating away at my insides.

When the speed stopped working, I started drinking. Actually, I was already drinking, but I took it to another level. Drinking made me feel one of two ways. It made me feel pretty and it made me feel I didn't care. But it wasn't enough. I did not understand why I thought collecting Crown Royal bottles was cute, but I did. What's worse is I couldn't see that it certainly wasn't normal. I was then introduced to marijuana. I liked the way marijuana made me feel, but I couldn't get with how it made me eat.

All of these outside things I was using were all about trying not to deal with the person in the mirror. I think you should know why I hated myself so much. As hard as it was for me to write this, it's even harder because I have chosen to not share this with my mom. Mom, I do not want you to ever question whether you did your part as my mom. You did everything you were able to do and then some. Thank you for taking such good care of me and loving me. As I stated earlier, when I was about 8- or 9-years-old, I was molested by a girl who lived a few houses down from my grandmother who I spent most weekends with. Since I did not have any knowledge about sex, I believed her when she told me that sex meant "girls being with girls."

I knew somewhere inside of me what we were doing was wrong. I certainly could not tell anyone, because I was wrong for participating. This is where the shame began for me; this is where my hate for self began. This is where lying about me began, not just to people, but to myself. The voice inside of me needed to be shut down. When I started finding things outside of myself to help me do that, I over indulged to get what I needed. After that experience other things began to take place in my life that was a direct result of that one thing I felt I could not tell. That one thing that was not my fault. I was violated and did not know it. That one thing gave me the feeling that I needed someone to show me they liked me, because I didn't like me.

Admiration helped me feel good enough. At least until they decided to leave or our relationship changed. I look back over my life and sometimes think, *how did I not lose my mind?* As time went on, I started running from me in more ways than just using drugs and alcohol. I moved several times to other cities and states hoping these moves would allow my life to be better. But when I got there the only thing that had changed was the location.

Everything else was the same; I did not realize then that it would not change because the change that needed to take place had to happen inside of me. Until the day came that I realized this fact, I used drugs as if I were taking aspirin. When the "aspirin" stopped working the pain returned. I did not know what the pain was, I just knew something was not right. It could not be about the molestation because that was over and done with; no one knew what happened but me and her. So why was I in so much pain? I kept that secret up to the age of 28-years-old.

I was supposed to be in pain. For over 20 years I lived with this horrible secret and wondered why I hated me more than anyone ever could.

Along with all of the other experiences that came after that first experience, I believe there is another key reason that the pain increased in my heart and that key was the day I discovered my step-father was not my biological father. I remember the moment my life changed, the period of time I was molested and the day I was told that the person who I thought was my dad was not. That is a day I can see like it was yesterday. The minute it was confirmed that I had a father and my step-father was not him, I was devastated.

I immediately felt different, I no longer felt like the person I was prior to being told. I no longer fit in my family. I didn't know who I was anymore. My mom, dad and sister all had the same last name. I felt that if I could have that, I would truly be a part of what I wanted so desperately—being a real member of this family.

From that day I started a journey of attempting to fitting in. Not just with people outside of my home but within my home. I can remember asking my mom if we could change my name so that I could have the same name. I remember practicing writing my name to see how it would look being a part of the family. It never happened. I never talked about my feelings around this major event in my life for over 20 years.

Even writing this confirms even more for me how painful that was. Sometimes it still is. I'm sure there are some other things I could mention to attempt to indicate how these events can and do affect our lives in ways that we don't connect together.

I must let you know that I have a great relationship with my parents. Even my biological father and I have developed an amazing relationship. My step-father, came into my life when I was 2-years-old and I have always looked at him as my father. He raised me and did everything he was able to do, to assure my mom and I were taken care of. I love him very much and am so grateful for the relationship God has allowed us to have.

You must get assistance to understand what the sweeping has done, otherwise you will return to what you know. I was blessed to find a professional to help me walk through the things that were screaming in my head and as I began to uncover bits and pieces of items under my rug. I was granted a chance to quiet those voices in such a way that started me on a path towards the freedom God wanted me to have.

Often when we hear someone say words like "quiet the voices," we think that person is not all there. That is the kind of thinking that keeps us from getting the help we need. I am not mentally ill I just have some issues that made me feel ill mentally. Even in my life right now, sometimes I'm afraid to call someone and say, "I am not doing well today." That sounds like a normal statement but my ego and pride says, "If you say that they'll think something is wrong with you." That happens to many people. They put off making the calls they need to make for fear of what someone will think of them. Then as time goes on they get worse never better, and then the issue of mental health becomes real.

One of my greatest fears is to lose my mind, and I believe that is why I am so transparent about what is going on with me. I am so grateful to have at least one or two people in my life that are always willing to take my call. They have made it very clear that no matter what my fears are telling me, they never get tired of hearing from me. There isn't any reason for me not to call.

If you are anything like me you may be able to relate to the fact that I believe I am a person who feels very deeply for others and sometimes it does not feel normal. I know those feelings are good feelings and I have been running away from them all of my life. I was always told that I trust too much, I love too much, I talk too much, and I want to help people too much.

I ran from Renee' because she was just too much for me to handle. The more I ran, the more I hated me. I did not know how to be me, but yet I did not know how not to be me either. I did not just wake up one day and this was all revealed to me; it was as a result of a lot of work that I have come to this revelation. I did not and still do not like seeking help when I am going through something that I cannot figure out for myself. But my history has shown that when I have given myself the opportunity to allow someone to help me find an answer or solution I can live with, it has been for the better.

Getting help is not the taboo thing that people have made it out to be. It is a way for you to listen to yourself in a way that helps you better understand you. When I can do that, I better understand the choices I make. I can recognize what is generating the feelings I may be having. I can tell the difference between the realistic and unrealistic. Getting help has helped me to know that I am okay; I am not alone in what I have experienced.

Talking with someone is an opportunity to practice not allowing what others think of me to control any aspect of my life. The other thing I discovered once I told those things I swore I would never tell, I felt differently. The control those things had on me began to not be so powerful. It is my desire that you can find the courage to get the relief you can receive from discovering what type of effect sweeping issues under the rug has had in your life. Do yourself a favor and make just one appointment. Don't think about all the times you may have to go. Those times are not as important as making the first appointment.

1. Now that you have written a list and revisited what happened, let's take some time to see how those discomforts have affected your life. Remember I mentioned in the beginning of this chapter that we sometimes use outside things. Write a list of outside things you could say you use for comfort. This may take a minute because sometimes we don't realize we do it. It may feel like the norm, but if we are honest we may say something like, "When I am disappointed, a new pair shoes just fixes everything." No, not you, that's me. Find your own outside thing!

2. Next, ask yourself what is it in my head that I have played over and over, and felt there was no need to talk with anyone about it? If you are still ruminating over a situation that took place in your life, it is very possible it is affecting you in some way. It could be stopping you from allowing people to get close to you for

example. You may want to consider seeing someone to help you to make peace with the event or events you have tried to ignore.

NOTES

NOTES

FOUR

Moving Forward Facing Rather Than Sweeping

The previous chapters show what can happen to those of us who attempt to ignore the experiences we have had in our lives. I am one who wishes we could be washed clean of all the horrible things we have had to deal with over the years. Unfortunately, the reality is, washing them away is not possible, and trust me when I tell you that I am one who really attempted to pretend that I could remove these thoughts from my head, my heart, my life. No matter how much I tried those things would show up at the most inappropriate time.

Once, I was working for a major law firm in Los Angeles as a receptionist. I came to work one day with either a hangover or after an all nighter, who knows which. One of my duties was to do an overhead page for phone calls or visitors when an attorney was away from his office. Well I made the page to the General Partner, and somehow forgot to disconnect. Then I began to laugh and who knows what else I said for all three floors to hear.

The general partner called me and said with great disgust in his voice, "It is very unprofessional for the entire office to have to hear you laughing through the PA system." My response was one I realize today came from an old experience I had when one of my family members who I respected and loved dearly spoke to me in that same tone. It was even more unprofessional. I told him, "Oh well, I'm human," and hung up. Why was I surprised when my supervisor wrote in my evaluation, I was *"overbearing"*? Can you believe that? Me, overbearing! At the time I did not even know what the word overbearing meant. Webster says it means, "tending to overwhelm, harshly and haughtily arrogant." This was the only way I knew how to be in order to live with who my insides told me I was—a nobody.

Oh my, how I thank God for deliverance. This is the reason that finding the help needed to flatten out your rug is way more important than just trying to sweep things further under the rug. Without help, we might miss the blessings we could have experienced, due to those old messages we have been living by. If you don't believe me, let me share another example. When I graduated from high school, someone asked me what I wanted to study in college. I told them I really wanted a psychology degree. Their response to me was, "Oh, if you get a psychology degree, you will have to get a master's in psychology for it to be beneficial." That sounds like good advice right? Why did I interpret that statement as something I should not consider?

At that moment I had a discussion with myself and said, "Self, we need to choose another direction. You are not smart enough to get a master's degree!" I then proceeded to figure out for almost 20 years, something else that might take the place of my desire to major in psychology. I eventually came full circle and got my master's in psychology. I delayed my own destiny due to living by old messages.

One day I was asked "Why can't you be like your cousin, so and so?" This particular cousin was very smart and appeared to always do everything right. I didn't look like her, didn't get grades like her, didn't act like her. I never thought I was smart, or pretty and I didn't know how to carry myself. Therefore, I could not believe I could achieve an awesome goal of receiving a master's degree. Why? Somewhere in my mind I felt unworthy, not good enough, not smart enough; just not enough anything. I was still running away.

What is it about getting help that people run from? If it has anything to do with being ashamed of having to get help, if you are living with your past experiences those things are probably creating shame and guilt. You are already living with the very thing that you are trying to run away from. Not getting help is that false pride that tells you nothing is wrong. It says, *disregard the fact that you cuss out the lady in the grocery store for whatever reason.* It says, *it is normal to be in a room with 100 people and feel like you are alone.* It says, *it is normal to not like any authoritative actions from a male figure because you have felt abandoned by the men in your life.*

The messages your past tells you are messages to keep you in the sickness, in the misery, in the familiar. People don't seek help because of the fear of what it will take to be committed to the steps that must be taken for the help to be successful. Mostly, we don't seek help because we pretend we are comfortable in our own mess. This is when we hear people say things like, "That's just the way I am." When you have to announce that's just the way you are, that statement is a defensive one which indicates there may be something you might want to look at in yourself. To admit it would be too painful to revisit. It takes courage to examine yourself and admit that you need help.

The work that must take place is not easy but the payoff is FREEDOM! Freedom to be all that God has called you to be, and allow the blessings into your life, that are for you. You have lived in fear long enough, and now is the time to step out on faith and seek the abundant life that has been promised to you. What started my journey to getting help was, one day I was laying in bed and I opened my eyes and I saw the face of the person who molested me like she was right there. I remember sitting up scared and in fear. I cried myself back to sleep and the next day I was driving on the freeway and as I was transferring from one freeway to another, I heard myself say, "If you drive off this freeway right now it would really be okay." The next thing I heard was a scream coming from me. I immediately called someone who I knew would assist me in getting what I needed. A day or two later I was in a psychologist office beginning the process.

The process of looking at my history was an experience that was hard but really good.

So much of what I once believed I found to be untrue, and what I needed to do was see what my truth really was and live based on that truth. It took a lot of honest probing and willingness to look at things that brought about some real emotional feelings. They were very hard to express and revisit, but were taking a toll on how I functioned in my life each day. I see quotes and hear people say, "Let the past go." I agree but what makes it so difficult is until we become at peace with the past, letting it go is a difficult task. Sometimes I believe we think we have gotten over something when in fact all we have done is pushed it way down. It resurfaces when it is needed to either support an event happening in our lives or remind us of a painful experience we thought we had dealt with.

Will getting help make everything that is under your rug come out of hiding and be okay? I can't promise that, but what I can promise is your rug will get flatter, and the flatter it gets, the more freedom you will gain. This is part of the reason most of us do not seek the help available to us. We want instant microwave gratification, in and out type of service. A friend of mine quoted Dave Ramsey from a seminar she attended: "Steady and slow, wins the race." If you want the freedom that is long lasting, then I say to you "Steady and slow, wins the race."

Another important component is the person who supports you through this. I was always told, "Be careful who you share your life with, and who you allow to minister into your life." I have found that to be true. I am a person who wants to trust everyone until you give me a reason to not do so. Is that right or wrong? I don't know. I do know is when that works it works well but when it does not work, it really does not work well!

Sharing events that have hurt us in the past with the wrong individual is like re-living the event all over again. Today, when I share something with someone, I do not care what they do with it. Once it's out there it is nothing you can do to get it back. Therefore, my gauge is to always determine where I am with what I need to share. Is the person I am sharing with a person I trust and do they have my best interest at heart? This part of dealing with what's under your rug is very important; it is the thing that has the power to make you nail the rug to the floor. How do you find them? They probably already exist in your life. But if not, then do what I did ...pray.

I asked God to show me the people He prepared for me to go through this process, and I don't think I have to tell you, HE did! There are literally four people who know things about me that no one knows and they have loved me, ministered to me and nurtured me through every step. These are the people that whether I am in their presence or not, they know when something is not right with me.

It is as if God has placed radar in them that says, "Call Renee, she needs you." I thank God for them. These are the people who tell me the truth, even when the truth may hurt. I believe and live by what the Bible says in John 8:32, "And you will know the truth, and the truth will set you free."

I know people God has blessed me with live their lives based on the Word of God therefore their counsel always comes from that basis, the truth. Ask God to lead you to your assigned angels, they are waiting for you. Are you now wondering what is going to happen once you pull this rug up and start the work for you to live this life God has ordained for you? I can't guarantee what it will be like for you, but I can certainly tell you what it was like for me. I initially felt some relief, but once the process of stirring up the stuff I had swept began, I realized how the pain under there had multiplied by 10. No wonder I reacted the way I have to many events most of my life, no wonder I could not stand to look at myself in the mirror, and no wonder I could not allow a man in my life who would stay. Oh, I didn't tell you about that? I could not allow a man in my life who would stay, because I was living with the belief that he would leave. Therefore, I *always* chose men who were very much unavailable emotionally and could not stay even if they wanted to. Wow... where did that come from?

As a child not understanding or not knowing everything about why my biological father was not present in my life, I grew up thinking, believing and feeling abandoned. Those feelings filtered over into relationships and not just relationships with men. I did not have genuine friendships either. I associated with people but when I look back over my life, I don't have the memories I often hear others talk about. Like when they discuss their childhood friendships and the things they did together. Even as a child I could not allow people into my life.

As I have worked through the old beliefs and affects my life has had on me, I have obtained some great memories in my adult life. God has blessed me with an awesome husband who loves me very much. He is not perfect, (thank God) but he is perfect for me. He wants to stay; he has no desire to not be available for me. He wants what's best for me and attempts to make sure that happens in the best way he knows how. I love him very much and thank God for allowing me to share my life with an awesome man and feeling greatly loved. I have to admit it took me a minute to get where I am in our relationship because of where I was emotionally.

I am so grateful that Andre' Daniels has held enough love and patience for the last 15 years. to trudge this road to my happy destiny.

1. Who do you say you are to yourself? Do you believe it?

2. How many real friends do you have in your life? If you had the courage to look back at each of your intimate relationships you could really learn so much about the mates you have chosen in your life. If you think you can handle it, it would really help you in ways you would not believe.

NOTES

NOTES

FIVE

It's All About Freedom, Your Freedom!

What has this been all about? What is it that I have been attempting to convey in the previous pages? I have wanted you to know there is freedom available to you if you want it, and the only person who can give it to you is you. I do understand that the steps you may have to take seem like a lot to consider. But if these steps are going to provide you with true freedom does it really matter that you may have to be a little uncomfortable to be free? In the end you may even find that your uncomfortableness is the thing that leads you to the purpose God has ordained for your life. Whenever I attempted to think about what God has ordained for my life, I had a real problem. I could not understand how God would allow me to go through the many things I have experienced. Then I would feel even worse, thinking I was questioning God concerning why He allowed these events. God eventually revealed to me the purpose for the events that have taken place in my life, and I am so excited that I did not give up prior to receiving that gift. Today my rug is flatter than it has been in a long time, and I would love to tell you there is absolutely nothing under it. But the truth of the matter is, I am not sure if the rug is no longer hiding any of my dirt. I know for sure that I have a sincere desire to address anything that may be revealed, should there be other issues existing I did not realize. It is my prayer that you will be able to attest to the same as you make this journey to your ultimate freedom.

It is my prayer that you will not allow fear to stop you from taking the steps necessary, to acknowledge that somewhere in your life you may have done just a little bit of sweeping. What are those steps? The first step has to do very much with an old saying, "To thine own self be true." This is a road that does not initially benefit anyone but you, and if undertaken thoroughly, you will be an unbelievable blessing to others who cross your path. This is what God wants us to be ultimately. When you think about the people in biblical days, you must admit they did not always realize what God was doing in their lives. Nor did they give thought to how their testimonies would bless people for decades to come. I can bet my last dollar that the woman with the issue of blood had no idea how her suffering and determination to rise above her physical condition would be an awesome example of how to persevere in spite of what it feels or looks like.

The same can be said for each of us. I had no idea that any of what has taken place in my life would be a blessing to anyone. When I became sober, I was talking with what we call a sponsor, someone who in the end you realized was sent to you by God to help you learn how to walk your new life. At the time, my sponsor, TaShia, said to me, "One day you will be able to really bless someone with what you have been through." I laughed (like Sarah when God told her she would have a son). I could not see how my drug-addicted life and lifestyle would ever be a blessing.

As a matter of fact my plan was to never tell anyone about my alcoholism and I surely was not going to tell anyone what I did when I drank or used drugs. I really could not see how dancing on tables in a black outfit was going to bless another human being. I mean how was God going to use that? I could not see how being molested as a child would ever be something that when I shared it with someone who is struggling in that area would be able to walk away not feeling alone, hopeless, and like it was not their fault. But there is not much I have experienced that has not been exactly what my sponsor said it would be... a blessing!

When you are able to put a name to the dirt which has been swept under your rug, letting the Son's light shine on the issues that have been festering is the ultimate healing power. God's power will lead you to what is needed to place you on the path to your freedom. You will discover what it all means and how it has affected your life. Once the discovery has been made, discarding it is not what it sounds like. Webster gives the definition of the word discard as, "To cast off as useless or as no longer of service; to dismiss from employment, confidence, or favor; to discharge; to turn away."

Usually, we want to do the opposite of the definition. It is my hope that you will be able to learn from each experience in such a way, that it will become an arsenal of weapons to beat the enemy in his desire to deceive us with our past.

Instead we will use it to show that God is quite capable of doing something with what the devil meant for a disreputable bad and use that for an extravagantly outrageous blessing.

In order for you to be clear of what it is God would have you to do, prayer has to be a great part of your life. Communication with God is important in all areas if our lives. It is where the strength comes from to walk through the situations we find in our lives. Being prayed up provides the power to do what I believe is most important, and that is to write down what you think you see. Habakkuk 2:1 in the Message Bible says: "What's God going to say to my questions? I'm braced for the worst. I'll climb to the lookout tower and scan the horizon. I'll wait to see what God says, how he'll answer my complaint."

FULL OF SELF, BUT SOUL-EMPTY

Habakkuk 2:3-4 **says,** "And then God answered: "Write this. Write what you see. Write it out in big block letters so that it can be read on the run. This vision-message is a witness pointing to what's coming. It aches for the coming—it can hardly wait! And it doesn't lie. If it seems slow in coming, wait. It's on its way. It will come right on time. Look at that man bloated by self-importance—full of himself but soul-empty."

Being able to write or journal about your life does two things. One—it takes some of the sting out of what has been plaguing you for years. Two—it allows you to see your life for what it is and where your soul once felt empty, it can be filled with great joy.

Once you have prayed and began to journal, you will be in a position to put words to what you have been covering up all these years. It is my hope that you realize that your rug is not a literal rug. Your rug can be a number of things like fear, shopping, eating, drugs, alcohol, sex, workaholics, perfectionism, depression, bad body image, and low self-esteem, to name a few.

We tend to use many things that make us feel better temporarily. What happens with this temporal fix is it stops working to sooth the pain. What is worse is there is no time to pinpoint when they stop doing what they have been doing for years. That is a very critical intersection; that place between working and not working.

In that small space there has to be room for God to hold you when you are there. The items we used to feel better were once our friends and were items used from the outside in when we should be attempting to fix what is happening to us from the inside out. What would you prefer?

Throughout this book there has been a lot of talk about how there is a very profound way to free ourselves inwardly. Once there are words to help explain what has been uncovered, we are then able to express ourselves. It would be so wonderful to be able to say, now that we have the information we will understand the whole picture. For some people that may be true, but for most people, this is the place where bringing in a professional could save them from some possible painful days and nights.

Just because I have some information does not mean I understand how to use the information I have been given. I proved that when I talked about how I had to take algebra three times. I had the information but I had no clue what to do with it.

I thank God for creating the profession of psychology, it is a gift that most people frown upon because of the fear that it says something about them is broken or wrong. In fact, what is discovered is not necessarily broken or wrong, but misunderstood by the person needing help.

This is a part of the journey that allows you the opportunity to practice being honest with yourself. The mistake people sometimes make is they tell part of the truth and expect a whole solution. It is easy to tell the parts of your story that may leave your past out of the equation.

Shame and guilt are the components that makes it difficult to tell what you believe is your part in the situation. Not wanting to be judged makes us tell the parts that are easy for us. Being afraid of discovering we are wrong is another reason we tend to leave out vital information. This is why the field of psychology is important. It allows us to express what needs to be expressed with a person who doesn't have a stake in us or in what takes place in our lives. For those of us who find we need it, a psychologist/counselor is God's gift in guiding His children to finding a peaceful way of living.

This journey takes us to a place of moving past our fears to the truth and what is the truth? The truth is, God has a plan for each one of our lives and if we seek Him, we are given what is needed to be the men and women of God, He has planned for us to be. The ability to move past fears is the power to face life rather than sweeping what does not feel right under a rug. TD Jakes said something very powerful, "Fear never leads to a positive place." Therefore, I say, "Face everything and LIVE!"

NOTES

NOTES

FRIENDS' SPECIAL WORDS OF ENCOURAGEMENT

Esther Renee' Daniels is a woman of integrity, a woman of passion and she walks fully and completely in the amazing freedom that allows her to embrace the fullness of what God has planned for her life. And she believes that same freedom is available for you.

In her book, *What's Under Your Rug*, she outlines a poignant description of the reasons why "sweeping it under the rug" keeps us in bondage to our past and how it hinders the amazing future God planned out for us before the foundation of the world. What have you "swept under the rug" of your life? As many of us understand this idiom, Renee' will take us down the highways of her own life on which we will discover that we are not alone.

There are many secrets in our families that have been "swept under the rug."

There are many disappointments and struggles that we have faced in our own personal lives that have been "swept under the rug." As you read through the pages of this book, you will be empowered to lift up that rug and deal with the dirt of your past. God has already given us strength for the battle which will carry you through every moment of the journey.

I did just that for a very long time in my own life with a very hurtful situation from my childhood. The seed of rejection and disappointment was planted at a young age and as I grew up that seed grew up as well. So, as you will discover in this book, when we hide our hurt and pain it doesn't go away. It just begins to grow bigger and bigger. It's been said that what we don't confront, we cannot conquer and such is true when we sweep things under the rugs of our lives. In this book, Renee' will remind us of an amazing truth in the Word of God that says, "All things work together for good to those who love God and are called according to his purpose" (Romans 8:28).

Therefore, every challenge that we face in our lives will be used by God to propel us into our true destiny that He planned for our lives. I challenge you to lift up that rug and begin to face all of the ugly, dirty things that lie under it and watch God do amazing things in your life.

True freedom is a treasure that you can have. I can remember the first time I met Renee and had a chance to really sit down and get to know her. She is the epitome of TRUE FREEDOM in Jesus. It was evident from the onset of our conversation that there was nothing under her rug. She has truly inspired me and I know she will inspire you. You will gain strength, courage and a level of determination you have never known before through the powerful insights Renee shares in this book.

Every word will empower you to LIVE Again with Purpose and Passion!! I encourage you as you begin reading this book to determine in your heart that you will complete it. Determine that you won't allow anything to stop you from fully embracing the True Freedom that is waiting for you.

You will then be able to Embrace Your Full Self, Express Your Full Self and LIVE like you never have before! Go Get Your Freedom!!

—Barbara Henderson,
Inspiring Moments: Inspiring
Your Life—Empowering Your Dreams

"What know ye not that your body is the temple of the Holy Ghost which is in you, which ye have of God and ye are not your own? For ye are bought with a price, therefore, glorify God in your body, and in your spirit, which are God's" (1 Corinthians 6:19-20). Ungodly alliances, ungodly attachments, ungodly mindsets, ungodly thoughts; what lives in your house under your rug? Life's most complicated issues are often a direct reflection of what we allow to live in our temple; our house. Friends and relations who mean us no good, negative self-talk, and attitudes that stop us before we even get started, all clutter our existence with mindsets of unclean thoughts, convoluted ideas, and clouded vision.

Our temple, our house, has been soiled by the issues of life. We've allowed the enemy into our abode through bad relationships, poor choices, and misguided steps. We've given him permission to destroy our habitat and mess up our house.

The trash has piled up producing a heap of unwanted debris crowding out all the valuables we've stored on the inside. Doubt, fear, lust, resentment and jealousy, shaped by traumatic experiences of divorce, death, years of abuse, bankruptcy, rape and other tragedies of life, have left us with pain we can't describe—a purpose in peril.

Hoarding disappointment, bitterness, anger and self-defeat we find ourselves unable to dig our way out so we just sweep it all under the rug.

It's time to clean out the clutter; time to get rid of the confusion, the disorder, the chaos. Esther Renee' Daniels has masterfully provided the tools necessary to get rid of the dirt we've allowed to build underneath our rug. Esther uncovers the mess and delivers a message of hope, deliverance, and breakthrough by the power of the One who is the Master Cleaner!

Good job Esther and thank you so much for this on time contribution of literary genius that is sure to set the captives free.

—Cheryl Lacey Donovan,
Pastor & Author

***

What's Under Your Rug is a wonderful book that points you to God's word to see what God says about you and encourages you to have hope for healing and freedom.

Esther Renee' Daniels offers steps to assist in the journey through her love and compassion assuring us that she's walked in our shoes and can relate without judgment. An inspirational and effective book that is a great resource for anyone ready to take their relationship with God to another level.

—Cynthia A. Patterson,
Founder & CEO DOVE Ministries, Inc.
Author of the book, It Had to Happen—
Understanding that everything you go through
in life is for God's purpose.

***

A couple of months ago, I went into the office on a Sunday afternoon to organize my desk following an office move. Little did I know that I was about to face one of my greatest fears, and that was being stuck in a dark elevator alone. Upon entering the elevator everything was great, but then once the door closed, the elevator began to move slowly and then stopped in between floors. All of the power shut down and there I was stuck, with no air and no lights. It was pitch black and I was all alone.

I felt as if the walls were coming in on me. My heart began to pound harder and harder as I felt along the walls to find the emergency call button. Finally, I was able to call security for help, but they told me it would be a while before the elevator repair guys arrived. I knew the only way I could make it out of this horrible situation without passing out, was to remain calm, take deep breaths and pray until help arrived. After about 15 minutes, the lights came on, I felt air and suddenly the doors came open. I was so relieved and thankful that ordeal was over. I took a mad dash out of the elevator only to meet several security guards waiting to call paramedics if necessary.

After submitting an incident report, I realized that I needed to get back onto the elevator to go up to the 24th floor where my office is located. As I approached the elevator, I found myself fearful that I had to enter it again. I grabbed a seat in the lobby to gather myself. It was then that I realized fear had gripped me more than I knew. Although I think of myself as a faith-filled Christian, I couldn't bring myself to face the fear of getting back onto the elevator again and potentially being stuck.

Well, to fast forward, I'm using the elevators again multiple times a day. When I enter the elevator, those that I ride with have no idea of my horrible experience and the fear that I've had to overcome regarding getting stuck in an elevator. As I began to read this dynamic book by Renee', I compared my elevator experience to that of men and women who are going about their daily lives emotionally trapped from negative experiences from their past. No one seems to know that they are an emotional wreck because they cover it well. They've tidied up and swept their "dirt" (past negative experiences) under the rug, never receiving the emotional healing, forgiveness, peace and joy that God has made available to them. In other words, they stay stuck in a dark elevator of life. Just like I had to go back into that elevator and face my fear, there are many who have gone through life with a mountain of emotional hurt and pain that they've refused to deal with and therefore, they remain stuck in their emotional prison of pain.

In this book, Renee shares many of her personal experiences, openly, candidly and from her heart. She uncovers events from her past that held her in emotional bondage. She emphasizes the importance of dealing with your past so that you can receive true freedom and embrace your future. As I read through the manuscript, I could identify events from my past that held me emotionally captive at one point in my life. It was not until the word of God became real to me that I discovered my true worth and identity. Then, I came to accept God's forgiveness and His unconditional love for me. The dirt that was under my rug was exposed and swept clean and now those experiences are no longer an embarrassment or hindrance to my progression, but rather a testimony of God's faithfulness in my life. Renee' is a beautiful woman of God and her life is a testimony of what it means to BE FREE! She walks you through how you can experience true freedom in life by facing your fears, exposing them, taking action to overcome them and learn from them. Get ready to walk into your freedom.

—Kendra Y. Adams

***

What's Under Your Rug is a perfect title for a healing read. Author Renee' Daniels has shared her journey to healthy esteem and God -given freedom buy uncovering past hurts and challenges. When I met her over 12 years ago she was a reserved, administrative professional with many gifts waiting to be used and talents lying dormant. I am honored to be considered one of her mentors, business partners and friends. While combing through cobwebs and clearing out the clutter, she tells of her constant pursuit for excellence in education, health and family commitment. Mrs. Daniels paints such a vivid picture of how uncovering the pain of you past can make you bitter or better. Her story ends with better. Congratulations Esther Renee' Daniels, I am so godly proud of you.

—Pastor Yolanda Carroll, Co-Pastor
Abundant Love Church, Houston, Texas &
Founder, DNA Ministries

BIOGRAPHY

Minister Renee' Daniels is a member and minister at The Fountain of Praise, under the leadership of Senior Pastor Remus Wright and Co-Pastor Mia Wright. Renee', as most of her friends call her, is always on a mission to spread God's word. She is a teacher of the gospel, a chemical dependency counselor and life coach. She holds a master's degree in psychology and has been blessed to utilize her gifts serving adolescents with mental illness and substance abuse. Her goal is to become God's best clinician and minister in order to serve his people where it hurts mentally and to help others to grow spiritually.

She is the founder of Titus Works Ministries, a vision she believes was downloaded specifically to her from God. This ministry has been created to spread the word freely to ages 25 and up. Titus based on the Word of God in Titus chapter 2, teaches us that the old shall be there to guide the young into a better life with Christ. Renee' has been blessed to counsel, motivate, inspire and encourage others that they can too, be a living testimony.

She gives 100 percent to everything she is asked to do for others. With all of that said, the most important thing she would like for you to know about her, is she loves God with all of her heart and wants nothing more than for God to be pleased with everything she does. To learn more about Renee' visit: http://www.titus2empower.com

MORE ABOUT THE AUTHOR

What can you say about a sister that has a big heart? As I remember where we were in our lives when we first met and see where we are today, our accomplishments are a testimony to the power of God! What word do I think of when I say, "Esther Renee' Daniels"? I think of determined! Renee' did not allow any of her challenges to hold her back. In fact, she's using them as stepping stones which have led to her writing this amazing piece, *What's Under Your Rug?*

There is no doubt that this book will be a bestseller and that it will help many people overcome so much in their lives. One thing about Renee' as we call her, is she sincerely cares about people and their betterment. Launching her non-profit ministry, "Titus Works," in 2011 prepared her to write her story of challenge, victory, and triumph.

Renee' is determined! She is determined to please God, determined to do it with excellence, determined to help as many people as she can and finally, determined to live the calling upon her life. The key and the secret to being deter-mined is that you must be UNSTOPPABLE and you must learn to live a life of faith governed by God! Renee' has done that!

Renee', one thing one of my mentors shared with me was that you don't have to get it right, just get going and everything else will fall into place for you.

Much love and success to you and much success with this wonderful masterpiece!

Michelle R. Harden,
The Brand Master
Author of Whatever You Do Brand You